TO BE

DELONDRA ELLIS

Book Cover Design: Prize Publishing House

Printed by Prize Publishing House, LLC
in the United States of America.

First printing edition 2025.

Prize Publishing House
P.O. Box 9856, Chesapeake, VA 23321
www.PrizePublishingHouse.com

ISBN (Paperback): 979-8-9925617-0-8
ISBN (E-Book): 979-8-9925617-1-5

"Behold, I was shapen in iniquity; and in sin did my mother conceive me."

– Psalm 51:5, KJV

It began with an inappropriate touch that brought confusion and questions to my mind. I was robbed of all my blessings from the only wise God, or better yet, they went dormant. I had no sense of direction or who I was or was to become because of insecurities and misunderstandings. The hand of the Lord had blessed me to be a happy, fortunate girl who was envied because of all the good things that made me prosperous. As I grew older, I denied all of that because I didn't know how to accept the good things about myself. I didn't want to be envied; that didn't feel good; I wanted to be loved and liked, but I didn't know how to be.

I thought I was supposed to be a different person because people didn't accept or like me for who I was. I would deny or try to hide my blessings from people; in other words, I didn't accept a compliment well. I would act as though it wasn't anything, or I'd say something negative about myself to take away from the compliment. I even tried to change my natural walk because I had a natural twist that brought attention to myself, and I didn't like attention to myself. I self-sabotaged myself, and even after doing that, I still wasn't liked by so many or loved; I was only judged.

Since I have come to know better, that is, to appreciate all the blessings that I was blessed with, I have repented for denying the hand of the almighty God on me and my blessings. I now say, "Lord, show me who I am," and then I confess who I am. I say, "Lord, show me more gifts from you," and I ask that you, Heavenly Father, touch me again!

CHAPTER
One

I grew up in the country—I was literally a country girl. When I was around five or six, "Big Momma," asked my mother if I could come live with her because Papa had passed away, and she was going to be living alone. So, Momma agreed, and I became Big Momma's company (lol). I lived with her until her health began to fail, preventing me from staying with her and her from living the country life anymore.

While growing up as a young girl, I never thought of myself as a pretty girl but as an "ugly duckling" because I was dark-skinned or too brown; I had sandy-colored hair that was thin and short. I compared myself to my sister, who was lighter skinned than I, and everyone thought she was cute. She was cute, chunky, and cuddly with light skin; she was the baby of the three of us. One of our babysitters called her Winnie the Pooh; that's how cute she was. I have one brother who is the second-born.

When I was in grade school, maybe first or second grade, my teacher would call me "Delightful Delondra." It is funny how that stayed with me all these years, not considering how I really felt about myself; however, she saw something about me that was just that, one of those hidden blessings that someone else saw that I didn't recognize or feel. Still, God did as well, and He caused her to see it, too. Delightful means to bring pleasure or joy - a blessing from the almighty God! But deep inside, I didn't feel it.

CHAPTER
Two

It began with an inappropriate touch that violated me by tainting the true meaning of love and affection. I believe I was about nine years old when my life and development were disrupted. This touch disrupted the purity of love and my relationship with a loved one, as love was entirely stripped from the situation. I didn't understand what it felt like to let love affectionately take control because I was too preoccupied with avoiding unwanted touches or misguided actions. I believed that allowing or expressing my love affectionately would imply "it's okay" or that I accepted their actions, so I rejected and tried to ignore the person in every way I could!

There was never any actual intercourse, just gestures, fondling, and hints. I remember going to school one day with swollen eyelids from crying all night and not understanding why. After denying my own pleasure and enduring his anger and frustration, it bothered me to the point of tears. Yet I kept the secret, pretending as if nothing was happening, trying to be a normal kid.

I grew up filled with fear, insecurities, and a long list of other feelings. Despite the confusion and doubt, I tried to hide this action or touch because it was embarrassing, and I didn't want my loved ones to know; I didn't want to hurt them.

I was robbed of my innocence, of what true and pure love is and is meant to be, so I went through the early years of my life with false notions of love. Love, in a sense, became less beautiful to me. I kind of stumbled upon real love—the true meaning of it—when I met and fell in love with my husband.

CHAPTER
Three

I had boyfriends as I grew up during my preteen and teenage years. I was never promiscuous but very particular about who I liked. I focused solely on relationships with the opposite sex, motivated by a desire to make a statement that "this is how it's supposed to be," or in other words, "I'm supposed to be in a relationship" or to experience an "Eros-type love with my boyfriend." Eros refers to romantic and passionate love (of the body). I never understood how it could be confused or misused, but in my case, it was, so I aimed to clarify or demonstrate it by being intentional about having a "boyfriend" but being particular.

As I grew into my preteen and teenage years, I felt misunderstood and disliked. People judged me, thinking I had an attitude and believed I considered myself better than others, but that couldn't be further from the truth. The reality is that I was just a confused, insecure, and hurt young lady trying to find my own path and discover who I was while seeking a better life. I held a secret that was too embarrassing to reveal, and I was only trying to fit in with my peers because their lives seemed normal, so I was trying to find my place.

I had awesome classmates; some went on to have great careers, while others didn't (including me). I didn't know what I wanted to do career-wise, nor did I have a clue; I just wanted to lead a normal life with ordinary emotions and a typical lifestyle. One of the biggest mistakes I made was not planning for my future or having dreams or ambitions.

CHAPTER
Four

The part of my life that wasn't whole or complete was paused when I met and fell in love with my current husband. He became my "everything!" I planned my future entirely around him; I saw no future without him! I didn't want further education; I was done with school, mainly because I didn't like it and didn't appreciate its advantages.

This man captured my entire attention. His voice was soft-spoken and smooth, and he was good-looking. What really caught my attention was that he was a military man still on active duty at the time. Back in the 1980s, having a car was a BIG plus, and he had one! I only wanted a future and family with him. I saw and fell in love with a man who was different from the other relationships I had in the past, so how could it not work?

I've realized since then that allowing someone to take your entire focus isn't healthy. There's nothing wrong with being in love, but ensure it's with someone who can uplift you in ways that foster growth for your spirit, mind, and future. The word of God in St. John 15:12-13,

KJV, states, "This is my commandment, that ye love one another, as I have loved you. Greater love hath no man than this, that a man lay down his life for his friends."

We got married, and I started to notice signs of infidelity. At the same time, I recall him doing beneficial things as the head of the household, like stocking our cabinets and refrigerator with groceries, thanks to the benefits of his adulterous relationship. However, due to our immaturity, his greed, and our shortcomings as a young couple, along with the fact that he was lured by lust and had many temptations available, he didn't resist.

So, here we are! I ended up raising three babies who were born 13 and 16 months apart. It was a lonely, isolated journey filled with shame about being alone and the feeling that I had lost what I thought was my everything.

For a brief moment, the thought of ending my life crossed my mind, but because of God's love and the realization that my life is worth living, He spared me! Praise God!

This is how I was led to the Lord; I gave my life to Christ!

During this relationship, the Lord saved me from making a huge mistake that could have led me away from my children if I had followed through with the process.

CHAPTER
Five

One night, I was with a family member of his who had convinced me to take her pistol and confront him and his adulterous partner. However, before I could leave the neighborhood, an act of God occurred. Somehow, my muffler got dragged down from under my car while I was on my way to him. Thank you, Lord!

There were several occasions during our marriage when I was harassed by his adulterous partner as if she were his wife; it was the craziest thing! I often wondered why this was happening to me since I didn't know her personally at all. I felt confused, ashamed, and lost at times, not knowing what to do because I had lost my mom, and in my mind, they were my future. But I held onto the Lord, and He held onto me.

The Lord brought me through all of this, and there was loneliness and incompleteness because my heart was broken and because I wasn't my husband's choice at that time; he left me no choice but to divorce him.

The word of God was given to me in my

situation from the book of Isaiah 54:6-8, KJV, "For the Lord hath called thee as a woman forsaken and grieved in spirit, and a wife of youth, when thou wast refused, saith thy God. For a small moment have I forsaken thee; but with great mercies will I gather thee. In a little wrath, I hid my face from thee for a moment; but with everlasting kindness will I have mercy on thee, saith the Lord thy Redeemer."

CHAPTER
Six

I was taken further down the road to another relationship and marriage. In that marriage, I found myself subject to my husband in a way that required me to work and earn my own money. I was convinced that we were to have a joint account; however, upon doing so, I wasn't allowed to withdraw funds because my paycheck was solely used for the bills, leaving me with nothing for myself.

Consequently, I had to ask him for money to support myself and my children. I became entirely dependent on him for everything. I felt I had no voice because nothing I said seemed to matter. Whenever I did speak, my words would be twisted and taken the wrong way. Therefore, my only means of communication during that relationship was essentially through letters, as it felt safer for me, and I was determined not to keep my feelings bottled up.

More than a decade ago, I realized it wasn't safe to hold in my feelings, so the Holy Spirit led me to put them on paper to release them for peace of mind and communication. After 11 years of being unable to fall in love with this man, I wondered why. I completely lacked a voice as his helpmeet and wife.

It all came to light when my children's father returned to their lives. I realized I was still in love with him, my first husband. Those true feelings were awakened suddenly! Only after I recognized my ongoing love for him did I understand why I couldn't fall in love with my current husband at that time, even after marriage and believing I would grow old with him.

I often questioned myself, "Why can't I fall in love with this man?" Even after doing everything I knew to do—being faithful, submissive, and trying to communicate, albeit limited verbally—to no avail, it didn't work. It was simply the fact that my heart belonged to someone else. The feelings I thought were gone were, in fact, only lay dormant; they were ignored and suppressed. I didn't realize how powerful true love really was. So here I was, married to one man and living in a whole different city. Eleven years in a completely different life and relationship, yet I find myself in love with another man who is also my first husband and the father of my children.

So, I asked, "Lord, what should I do?" I began to seek the Almighty God through prayer for His guidance. I have always tried to be true to what's in my heart, but in this case, it felt unusual and out of order, and I couldn't ignore that feeling. I tell you, it was one of the most miserable feelings I've ever experienced. I knew the Lord didn't want me to live this way.

CHAPTER
Seven

Things had begun to go downhill in the marriage due to everything that was happening, so I started preparing for a divorce after he distanced himself from the relationship by moving out of the house, as he believed he was teaching me a "lesson."

I traveled back home in the spring to apply for shelter for my children and me so we could have our own space. By the end of May, we had moved back home. My confirmation of separation was his moving out before we even discussed divorce, and I did not share the feelings I was experiencing. I was approved for my place back home before we packed up and traveled, and things were falling into place. The Lord moved on the heart of a dear sister in Christ, prompting her and her husband to come to help us pack the U-Haul, just another way the Lord was working on my behalf during this move.

I chose to move back home because I knew I could improve my financial situation in a more familiar environment, so I started all over again. It was kind of like being taken back to where it all began—the beginning. If I learned anything, it's that the Lord is in control, and His will, no matter the situation, will be done in my life!

After returning home and getting a divorce, my first husband and I began working on our future together. He told me he was ready to change and that he would say yes to Almighty God. Did that happen? No! So here I was, in love with an unsaved man—not just any man, but my first husband, first love, and the father of my children—misled and lied to because I believed he would change. I tried being in other relationships to forget about him, but to no avail; they didn't work. Even though he was still living with his adulterous partner, I still couldn't move on with my life because he had my heart still.

He and his adulterous partner started having problems in their relationship that led to their breakup. He ended up moving in with me and our daughters. I thought, now I have him to myself, and it would be how it's supposed to be. I was still in my feelings because

I believed my heart wouldn't lead me astray. There were trials to face concerning us because, at the time, I was the only one working, making barely minimum wage, as he was disabled and waiting for disability approval. We still weren't remarried. We were living in the projects for the second time.

Things weren't coming together as well regarding the man I was still in love with—my first husband, my children's father, the man who said, "I'm ready to change my lifestyle."

CHAPTER
Eight

Eventually, I improved my credit to the point where I could purchase another vehicle and my own home, allowing me to move out of low-income housing. To God be the Glory! At the same time, the Lord provided me with a better-paying job that offered more than I had ever earned, enabling me to afford a mortgage and a car payment. All these things came together simultaneously.

Unfortunately, things didn't come together as well for the man I realized I was still in love with - my first husband, the father of my children, who had promised to change his lifestyle and had moved in with me. I found myself confused about our relationship moving forward despite having been in previous relationships that didn't work out. However, he was there with me and helped me move into my new home. My relationship with the Lord was very important to me. I wanted to maintain a right fellowship with Him going forward; I knew that living together without being married wasn't right in His eyes. Because of this, and because I was still in love with him, we remarried in holy matrimony on August 22, 2009. I can say there are still some uncertain days, but I do believe there is a purpose.

I tell women who have faced obstacles in love that it is possible for true love to find you. True love found me.

I'm very thankful for the goodness of Jesus. I call these things the "goodness of Jesus" because they led me to salvation, and today, I'm free and ready to live my life the way it's supposed to be lived.

CHAPTER
Nine

The confusion, insecurities, and "the secret" set my whole life back, but I learned valuable lessons throughout it all, the most important of which was wisdom. If you're not going to learn or allow wisdom to emerge in your life, then all your trials and experiences are in vain. Now that I know how to do so, I'm using every disappointment and hurtful experience I have faced to elevate my mindset.

Before I understood the purpose of my life, I thought everything that happened to me was meant to hurt and that no one was there for Delondra. I held pity parties and wished to be like others because I certainly didn't want to be myself. Their lives seemed so much better—together, confident, and happy. What I didn't realize was that the Lord was preparing me through those experiences I was going through. I've always heard that you go through challenges so you can help others, but I had no idea it would lead to my writing a book to share my personal encounters.

When I turned 50, I realized I had an unusual life due to the things that had happened to me. After everything that occurred, including some things I didn't mention, I didn't lose my mind or my identity. It's only through the grace and mercy of Father God and the redemption offered by our Lord and Savior Jesus Christ that these experiences didn't consume me to the point of destruction.

I pray and hope that the things I've shared will inspire others to share and realize it's okay to tell the truth about yourself because the truth will set you FREE!

I am FREE!